MW01488733

Early Retirement Solutions:

How Much Money Do I Really Need to Retire

& Achieve Financial Independence?

By: D.J. Whiteside

First Edition

Copyright © 2016 by DJ Whiteside

Disclaimer and FTC Notice

No part of this publication may be reproduced or transmitted in any form or by any means, mechanical or electronic without permission in writing from the publisher.

This book is for entertainment purposes only. The views expressed are those of the author alone and should not be taken as expert opinion, instruction, or command. The reader is responsible for his or her own actions.

While the author is not a certified or trained financial professional, all attempts have been made to present this content to the best of our understanding. Neither the author nor the publisher assumes any responsibility for errors, omissions, or contrary interpretations of the subject matter herein.

Neither the author nor the publisher assumes any responsibility or liability whatsoever on the behalf of the purchaser or reader of those materials. Any perceived slight of any individual or organization is purely unintentional.

Adherence to all applicable laws and regulations, including international, federal, state, and local governing professional licensing, business practices, advertising, and all other aspects of doing business in the US, Canada, or any other jurisdiction is the sole responsibility of the purchaser or reader.

Sometimes affiliate links are used within this content. This means if the reader uses a link and decides to make a purchase, the author may be entitled to monetary compensation. All affiliate links were researched and believe to be of the highest quality service. Please make sure you understand any financial obligations before making a purchase online.

Table of Contents

Get Our eBook FREE!

As our way of saying thanks, we've got a great ebook that is all yours for FREE! Please go to MyMoneyDesign.com to download your complimentary copy of **How to Plan Your Financial Freedom**.

In this book, we'll introduce you to the step-by-step process of coming up with a strategy to get your finances to a point where you no longer have to depend on your job for money. This will give you the chance to do whatever you want to do: Retire, travel, take on new hobbies, try a new profession, ... or just about anything else you can imagine!

In addition to the ebook, you'll also receive helpful updates from our blog. **Sign-up and download your free copy today!**

Introduction

Have you ever thought about "the number"?

You know ... the amount of money you'll need to save up in order to finally be *financially free*?

Sure you have! We've all given it some consideration at one time or another.

While most of us tend to work and save towards this goal with the best of intentions, one thing we often don't spend enough time thinking about is *the way* in which we'll put this money to use once we have it.

Why would that be important?

Because it can have a *tremendous* affect on how much we truly need to save. The difference between what you think you'll need and the "real amount" may shock you!

My Friend and I At Lunch …

Me: *I don't know. My wife and I will probably work another 10 years or so, and then we'll see. We might just retire after that …*

My friend: *Retire? How do you plan to pull that off? Did you guys suddenly become rich or something?*

[No, we didn't.]

Me: *Easy. We have a plan and stick to it.*

My friend: *Wow. Well, good for you! Unfortunately, my wife and I will probably work another 30 years or so until we're both old and grey.*

Me: *Why do you say that?*

My friend: *Because that's how long it will probably take us to save up a couple of million dollars!*

Me: *A couple of million dollars? That sounds like an awful lot. Why do you both think you need a couple of million dollars?*

My friend: *I don't know. Isn't that how much money you're supposed to have if you want to retire?*

How Do You Know "How Much" Enough Is?

A couple of million dollars ... huh?

A reply like that doesn't surprise me one bit. Most people have absolutely no idea how much they'll really need in order to be financially secure someday.

Don't feel bad at all if you're one of them. It's not exactly something you're taught in Kindergarten along with your ABC's and how to tie your shoes. On that same note, most high-schools and colleges offer nothing in the way of educating young adults about how to properly manage their finances. (Ironic since this would be the absolute optimal time to start putting compounding returns to work!)

No, instead we're lead to believe by popular media that our finances are an *extremely* complicated labyrinth where we're bound to make mistakes. Perhaps this is why the financial planning industry is in such ultra-high demand. At a staggering value of $49 billion per year, that's a lot of people who need help figuring out how to handle money!

To make the situation even more complex, what happens when you want to exit the rat-race ahead of your peers and retire early? How does that change the dynamic? How much extra money are you supposed to save now?

As someone who personally has a goal to be financially-free long before the norm, I can tell you that I completely feel your frustration when it seems that nearly every personal finance article available seems to cater to the status quo of working for 30 years and retiring after the age of 65.

Where are all the articles that talk about retirement by age 55, 45, or even 35? Where's the advice that shows us how to get there in 20, 15, or even 10 years from now?

The reason why goes back to the financial industry as a whole. After all, you don't grow to become $49 billion without doing some clever fear-marketing ...

Like my friend above, they've got the entire public believing their doom-and-gloom headlines that everyone is going to need at least "a couple million dollars" saved up in order to be properly prepared for retirement.

It's frightening. But not in the way that you're probably thinking.

Yes, it's true that most Americans are doing a poor job saving for retirement and are nowhere close to this goal. According to the latest Quarterly Retirement Snapshot from Fidelity, the fact that the average 401(k) balance of 10 years or more is only $251,600 shows that we are FAR from being prepared.

No, what bothers me is on the other side of the spectrum – the potential that other-wise responsible, working-class people might be possibly saving *too much* towards a finish line that's completely unrealistic.

The Dangers of Over-Saving

Saving your way to financial independence is not just some lofty goal. In order to hit your target, you first have to define exactly what that target is.

Unfortunately, like my friend above, we've all been "scared" into thinking that without a "couple of million dollars" that we'll spend our retirements being forced out on to the streets fighting alley cats for the best scraps of garbage to eat.

While some people would try to argue that you can never save too much money, I can think of quite a few reasons why it could potentially do more harm than good.

Over-saving can cause you to:

- Work more years than you really need to. With life expectancy only at 79, do you really want to work a day more than you absolutely have to?
- Put up with more crap and stress at your job than you should.
- Allow your health to go un-checked.

- Miss out on quality time and experiences with your family.
- Save excessively when a lower rate might have worked just fine.
- Live below your means when you probably didn't need to.
- Deny yourself and your family luxuries that you actually could have afforded.
- Take away from your hobbies and doing the things you truly love to do.

What should we really be focused on?

How about re-calibrating exactly what our savings targets are, or (better yet) could be!

What if instead of a couple of million dollars you would in fact retire comfortably with a goal of saving just one million dollars?

What if your number is really only $900,000? Or $800,000? What if it turns out you'd be fine with even less than that?

As I think you'll find out, it doesn't take NEARLY as much money as you think it does to retire early and be happy. A big part of how you come up with your number is by understanding the mechanics of how you'll get there.

And that's entirely what this book is all about!

What You're Going to Learn

We're going to be spending a lot of time going through the steps to define exactly what your "target" actually should be.

To do this, we'll be using proven methods and strategic research from some of the best and brightest in the retirement planning community. This will include conventional ideas, data from financial researchers, and lessons from real life people who have actually achieved financial freedom at a relatively young age.

Our goal, of course, will be to ***do more with less***.

By this, I do NOT mean to save the least amount of money possible. I mean to get the most amount of "value" out of your savings as you possibly can. (There's a big difference.)

We're going to do this by helping you understand what the different strategies will mean for you. Requiring a lower nest egg is just one possible outcome. Another could be more safety and confidence in knowing that your money will last. Or it could also mean starting your retirement from an earlier date.

Whatever factors are the most important for you will determine how it all comes together.

The best part: Everything we're going to talk about will apply to ANY stage of the financial freedom adventure: Regular retirement, early retirement, and anything in-between.

(By the way: I'll be using the word "retirement" loosely throughout this book. Please don't let it conjure up images of grey hair and discounted coffee. To me, being financially-free or the ability to be retired if you choose is all the same thing; no matter what age you achieve this. As I'll illustrate later, there are plenty of good examples of regular people who have figured out how to get there in their 30's and 40's.)

Ready to Find Out How?

Good! Then let's get started!

Chapter 1

The Mechanics of Financial Freedom

The concept of financial freedom is a pretty easy one to follow.

One of my favorite quotes on this topic comes from author Charles Farrell in his book "Your Money Ratios":

All decisions you make should help move you from being a laborer to being a capitalist. All of us are laborers. But as a capitalist, **you are not paid for the value of your labor, but for the use of your money.**

In other words, you could think of financial freedom is being the point at which you transition from someone who needs to work for money to being someone who's money works for them. Rather than going to work every day and getting a paycheck, all of the money you'll ever need will come from the assets you've spent your life accumulating.

So how does this work? How exactly does one become a "capitalist"?

The Retirement Equation

This may shock you, but at its core, retirement planning really simple. It really only comes down to three very important elements:

1. How much **income** you desire each year when you're retired.
2. The **withdrawal rate** or percentage of your money that you can reliably take out of your nest egg savings each year.
3. The size of the **nest egg** (the summation of all your savings for retirement).

Putting these three variables together, they relate to one another like this:

$$Income = (Nest\ Egg) \times (Withdrawal\ Rate)$$

Or, if you're interesting in understanding how much you need to save in your nest egg, then you can re-write the equation as follows:

$$Nest\ Egg = (Income) / (Withdrawal\ Rate)$$

These three factors are like a triangle. They constrain one another. You can't move one part without affecting the other two.

Example

According to the Census Bureau, the estimated real median household income in the U.S. was $54,462 in 2015. Because I like to use realistic numbers in my examples, we're going to round this number down to $50,000 and use it as our target retirement income figure all throughout the book.

Of course, the equations are simple enough that you will be able to do the same thing with whatever number is better suited to fit your specific needs.

If we generically assumed we could withdraw 5% from our nest egg each year, then the target nest egg that we'd need to save up for would be:

$50,000 / 0.05 = $1,000,000

Is That All There Is To It?

Of course not!

[If it was, then this would be a very short book.]

The thing about retirement planning (and especially early retirement) is that **it's not the equation that's hard, but <u>the meaning behind the numbers that's important</u>!**

I can't stress this point enough, and so I'll say it again.

Knowing what makes for "good" numbers is critical!

As we went through that simple example above, you probably had a lot of VERY good and completely valid questions:

- Is $50,000 enough retirement income?
- What if you need more?
- What if you could be happy with less?
- Is a withdrawal rate of 5% appropriate?
- How long will it last?
- Is it safe?
- How do we know?
- Where's the data to prove it?
- What sort of things do we have to invest in to make this all work?
- What about inflation?
- Is $1,000,000 a large enough nest egg?
- What if you could enjoy the same amount of retirement income with a lower nest egg?
- How much extra safety does saving more actually get me?
- Is it even worth the extra trouble?
- Will there be anything left to leave to my heirs?

- … any many more!

That's what the rest of this book is going to cover. We're going to explore each of these questions more thoroughly and really try to gain a better understanding of what numbers to use for each of these variables.

In the Next Chapter

To begin our exploration, let's first examine the "Income" part of the equation and better understand what our retirement income needs will actually be like.

Chapter 2

How Much Income Will You Really Need?

Imagine it's your first day of never having to work again. You've waited a very long time for this day! So now that it's here, what are you going to do today?

- Are you going to get some stuff done around the house?
- Maybe you're going to go play golf, or do that other hobby you like to do.
- Maybe you'll finally relax!

Now imagine a week has gone by. How many times have you:

- Ventured out?
- Gone out to lunch?
- Been to the store?
- Made purchases?
- Visited family or friends?

Now imagine it's been a year. How many:

- Trips have you planned?
- Places have you traveled?
- Projects have you started?
- Groups have you joined?
- Other things you've done to keep yourself busy and occupied?

Now for the not-so-fun stuff. How many times have you:

- Been to the doctor?
- Been to the dentist?
- Been to the hospital?
- Filled prescriptions?
- Had an x-ray?
- Had a surgery?

What about the number of times:

- The car had a problem and needed repaired.
- Something in the house stopped working.
- You had to get a new washing machine or refrigerator.
- You needed a new roof or had to fix a foundation crack.
- You had to handle some unexpected emergency.

Is your fixed income starting to feel a little constricting?

Being Realistic About Your Needs

Why am I asking you go through this mental exploration of ups and downs?

Because of this reason: It's very important that **your entire financial freedom plan is based on realistic numbers that you believe in**; not just numbers you think you can live with.

Make sure you really understand the difference between the two. I read blogs all the time where people seem to try to talk themselves into thinking that they can retire comfortably on some small amount of savings and will be happy living near poverty. Why? To me, it seems, they are more fixated on achieving the goal of early retirement rather than understanding what the goal really means.

Don't fool yourself into doing things backwards. It's a recipe for disaster!

Your retirement plan needs to be based on your spending habits and your lifestyle. It has to be reflective of the way that you actually want to live. People who have achieved financial independence stay that way because their plan was built to suit their goals rather than to simply reach some arbitrary number.

Depending on how much work you've already put into this topic, this mental exploration may also help you gain a better understanding of what retired life will actually be like.

For some people, you may have realized that your life in the future may require more money than you thought. But for other people, they may be surprised to find out that it could require less.

A Starting Point: 80%

Confused about where to take your first step towards gauging your retirement income?

Don't be. Financial research has shown that, on average, most people tend to live on roughly 80% of their pre-retirement income.

Why 80%? Because that's actually about how much you already live off of right now. Here's how they come up with that figure:

- Start off with 100% of your gross household pay.
- Subtract away 10% for your 401(k) contributions (if that's how much you contribute) since you won't be contributing to a 401(k) when you're retired.
- Subtract away another 7.65% for your FICA (Social Security and Medicare) taxes since you will no longer be paying those either once you're retired.

- Finally, subtract away another 5 to 10% since you will no longer have a lot of the same work expenses such as commuting, new clothes, dry cleaning, eating out at lunch, after work drinks, etc.

Remember: 80% is just another generic, average recommendation to give you a place to start.

To actually get a better idea of what will fit your specific needs, you'll need to create an estimated future budget ... and we're going to do that right now!

What Will Your Future Budget Look Like?

Grab a copy of your budget ...

(... you do keep a budget, right? ...)

Go through each expense category line by line. Adjust your figures based on what you *realistically* think they will be.

If they are more expensive then what they are now, don't worry. This is just an exercise; start it off with how you'd like it to be.

Expenses

Think about the categories that you might have in the future that you probably aren't accounting for today.

I can think of one big one: Health care. If you aren't paying for your medical expenses right now because your employer is covering them, then that will probably change. Whether or not Medicare exists in the future by the time you are able to retire early, there will more than likely be something similar to it. So for planning purposes, feel free to work it into your numbers.

What about extra money for travel? Now that you're financially free, you're probably going to want to get out there and see the world. And your pocketbook shouldn't hold you back from doing so!

Also, feel free to add in any extra new expenses you foresee. For example: If you always wanted to take up golf or learn to cook, those will both be great hobbies to learn. But they will not be free!

Do you have some sort of an idea of a monthly / annual figure?

Great! But we've got further to go.

Deductions
Now we're going to take some money off of that number you just figured out, starting with taxes.

Taxes. We haven't worked taxes (Federal or State) into our equations yet, and those will definitely need to be considered.

But here's the good news: There's a good chance that if you're planning to retire early and live off of less money than what you earn right now, you'll more than likely enjoy a lower effective tax rate.

Just so you know, when someone says you're in the 25% tax bracket, you don't calculate your taxes by simply multiplying your income by 25%. The U.S. tax system calculates your taxes using something called a "marginal tax bracket system".

All you have to do is take your desired annual income number, subtract away your standard deduction, a personal exemption for you and your spouse, and then you're left with your taxable income level.

Don't worry! It's not too hard to estimate them. But it is important that you do it the proper way.

(By the way, how would you like to pay zero taxes in retirement? Go to MyMoneyDesign.com and check out my post "The Ultimate Guide to How to Have a Tax Free Retirement " where I detail how to pull this off.)

Pensions. Next, you can deduct away any pensions or other guaranteed income from your annual desired income amount. Unfortunately for most people, unless you work for the state or a union that still offers them, this one won't apply.

Social Security. Despite what you may think, you are entitled to receive Social Security payments in the future if you have been paying into the system and meet their qualifications. Go over to Social Security's website and try out their free calculator to find out how much you and your spouse will qualify for.

Be mindful that after the year 2034, they only have enough funds to pay out 79 cents for every dollar you're entitled to. Even at this fraction, your Social Security income will be an important part of your overall retirement plan.

Please don't quite subtract this value from your annual total yet. Later on, I'll have some different and creative ways we can incorporate them into our strategy.

So ... What Is Your Final Target Number?

What number did you come up?

$100,000 per year? $10,000 per year? A million?

It doesn't really matter. Your plan is about YOU.

Please write that number down. Really! Write it down somewhere. Writing it down makes it REAL!

We're going to constantly be referring back to your target income. Then, near the last chapter, we're going to re-visit it and do some more things to refine it even further.

In the Next Chapter

Now that we have a retirement income goal to shoot for, the next logical question will be: *How does this number relate to my nest egg*? *How does saving and investing my money become a means for producing all the income I'll ever need – passively*?

You're about to find out!

Chapter 3

Your Nest Egg & Passive Income

If you don't recall your parents or grandparents ever fussing over 401(k)'s and how to save their money for retirement, there's a good reason for that: Most of them didn't have to.

In the last chapter, I briefly mentioned "pensions". All throughout the 1900's, a person typically relied on this thing called a pension to fund their retirement. This was an arrangement where as the employee worked, both the company and employee would save money together inside of a pool of money called the pension fund. At the end of some minimal number of years of service (typically 30), the employee would be offered the opportunity to quit working and start taking a steady stream of guaranteed payments from the pension fund for life. These payments would continue to flow and provide for their retirement needs for literally until they day they died!

(Here's a fun fact: Pensions were first introduced in 1875 by the American Express Company.)

However, since the 1990's, pensions have become like VCR's and CD's — they're dying out. They unfortunately proved to be too burdensome for most private companies handle. Instead, most private companies have now transitioned to a new type of retirement saving system called a defined contribution plan. These would be things like a 401(k), 403(b), or 457. As a supplement, the IRS also introduced IRA's.

This seemingly small shift did something dramatic: It transferred the burden of saving and retirement planning from the employer to the employee.

While this might seem like a negative, depending on how you approach it, **this could also be a unique opportunity to grow your fortune way above and beyond what you could with a pension!**

How so? Because you're allowed to save, invest, and grow your money however you see fit! Not according to how your employer or someone else dictates it for you.

You get to decide how to manage your nest egg.

What Makes a Nest Egg So Special?

As we learned in Chapter 1, your nest egg is an essential part of your retirement plan because it offers you the opportunity to become a capitalist. It gives us all the funds we'll ever need to support our lifestyle during retirement.

But a nest egg is something more than that ...

Your nest can also be used to effectively grow and even re-generate your funds even while you're making withdrawals.

The "Bucket" Analogy

Think of your retirement savings like water in a bucket.

Imagine there's a hole in the bottom of that bucket. That hole represents you taking out withdrawals to use for your living expenses.

Over time, all the water in that bucket is going to run out eventually.

How do we prolong this? By adding water to the top of the bucket to keep it fuller for longer.

Translation: We need to earn money on top of the money we already have.

How do we do this? With investing!

Let's illustrate the difference with an example showing how simple interest can prolong your savings.

Example

Let's say you saved up $1,000,000 and kept it in your local savings account earning no interest. Using our generic $50,000 target income figure, we could estimate that our money will last us $1,000,000 / $50,000 = 20 years. After that, we'd completely deplete our nest egg and have $0 left.

(Actually, if we count inflation, our money will last for fewer years than this, but for now we'll keep this example simple. More to come on inflation later.)

Now consider what would happen if you were able to find an online savings account that pays a fixed 2% interest. Using the NPER function in Microsoft Excel, we can easily calculate that our $1 million will now last you 25.8 years before the entire balance is completely depleted.

That little bit of interest just added almost 6 years of income to our lives!

How to Turn Your Assets Into Passive Income

That last example probably had you thinking: *What if that interest rate was even higher?*

If we were earning more interest than what we're withdrawing, is it possible that (in theory) we could simply live passively off of just the money we're making from the money we already have?

The answer: Absolutely!

Go back to our bucket analogy. To take this a step further, if you could fill the bucket with more water than what is being emptied out through the bottom, then not only would you never empty the bucket, you'd end up with a surplus spilling over the top!

In other words, if you had enough money, **you could feasibly live off of only the new money we're earning from our original money – passively generating all the money you'll ever need for the rest of your life!**

As we saw in the above examples, the key is to get better rates of return from "investing" your nest egg and letting it grow!

So how do you get a better rate of return on your investments?

Getting a Better Investment Return

At today's interest rates of 1 percent or less, a savings account is an extremely poor choice for your nest egg.

To get the most "bang for your buck", you're going to need to be open to investing in the market! By this, we mean investing in things like stocks, bonds, and other assets. These types of things can be easily purchased through the mutual funds you'll find in your tax-sheltered 401(k), IRA, or even in a regular taxable brokerage account with someone like Vanguard.

Mutual funds are free to move up and down in value as the market changes each day. Some years you might make a lot of money, and some years you might lose value.

But it's not as much of gamble as you may think. The good news is that, on the average, stocks and bonds tend to produce a net positive return over the long run. In fact, according to data compiled by NYU (as of the writing of this book), the markets have returned the following since 1928 on an average annualized basis:

- Stocks (S&P 500): 9.50%
- Bonds (10 Year T-Bonds): 4.96%

With returns like that, you've got a <u>much, much</u> greater opportunity for your nest egg to grow and sustain your lifestyle for the rest of your life!

Dividends

When we're talking about stocks, I should mention that there is a very easy, popular, and enticing way to passively generate income: Dividend stock investing.

Dividend stock investing is very attractive to many investors because not only do you own companies who are likely to appreciate in value, but you also get the extra, awesome benefit of receiving a physical "dividend payment" every quarter.

Similar to a savings account or bank CD, if you could build up a large enough portfolio, you could (in theory) simply live off of just your dividend payments and never touch the stocks!

Example

The current average dividend yield of the Dow Jones Industrial stock index is 2.75% (according to the Dogs of the Dow). If you had a million dollars invested in these stocks, you would receive $27,500 in dividend payments every year to use for your retirement.

Caveats

While I love dividend stocks and think they can be a very important part of your portfolio, I would not recommend that you rely on them solely. Just like a well-balanced meal will have just the right proportions of protein, carbohydrates, and fiber, your finances should also not be too heavy in any one type of investment.

In November 2012, Vanguard released a very informative publication on why something called a "total-return approach to investing" was better than one that simply chases yields or income (like a dividend income strategy). To sum it up, chasing too heavily after dividend yields can leave you over-exposed to one segment of the market where you might miss out on other growth opportunities such as capital gains. In addition, with historically low dividend yields, you either need a whole lot of principal to sustain the income you're looking for, or you open yourself up to more risky stocks that may or may not continue to pay that higher dividend you're after.

Therefore, for the rest of this book whenever we talk about stocks, we'll be referring to the S&P500 market index where you can rely on a healthy mix of both capital gains and dividends.

In the Next Chapter

Now that we have a better understanding of how a nest egg generates the retirement income we need, the next big question will be: *What proportion of nest egg should we have relative to our desired retirement income?*

In other words, how many times should we amplify the amount of retirement income we're after in order to make sure that we don't run the risk of ever running out of money?

Because of all the research that's available, we're going to spend quite a bit of time over the next few chapters exploring some different opinions about the concept of something called the "safe withdrawal rate".

What's a safe withdrawal rate you ask? ….

Chapter 4

The Safe Withdrawal Rate Concept

In the previous chapter, we learned how increasing your rate of investment return would help you create more passive income.

We looked at building a nest egg with assets that gave us a few different rates of return:

A) A bank CD at 2% interest per year
B) Bonds that earn approximately 5% per year
C) Stocks that earn approximately 10% per year

In other words, if you had $1,000,000, these assets could theoretically passively generate the following levels of income for you each year:

A) Bank CD: $1,000,000 x 0.02 = $20,000
B) Bonds: $1,000,000 x 0.05 = $50,000
C) Stocks: $1,000,000 x 0.10 = $100,000

While that might seem pretty obvious, one thing that people often forget is that a higher rate of return could also mean that we might not need as big of a nest egg.

Think back to our Retirement Equation from Chapter 1. If I wanted to create $50,000 per year of passive income, for example, that I could use to cover my living expenses, then using each of the rates above, all I would need to do is save up the following:

   A) Bank CD: $50,000 / 0.02 = $2,500,000
   B) Bonds: $50,000 / 0.05 = $1,000,000
   C) Stocks: $50,000 / 0.10 = $500,000

Now, let me ask you: *Which one would you rather save up?*

If you're like me, I'd much rather go the easy route and only save up $500,000 as opposed to $2.5 million!

As you can see, the withdrawal rate you choose can inversely amplify the size of the nest egg you need to save up. The larger the rate, the less money you're going to need to save.

For this simple example, our earnings rate = withdrawal rate.

But is it always? ...

Danger: Average Returns are Not the Same as Guaranteed Returns!

There's a very good reason I used the example above to make a point and lead you astray …

… nearly everyone makes that mistake when they first get into retirement planning!

(Even yours truly made this rookie mistake.)

What's more scary is that up until the 1990's, financial professionals, the people from that $49 billion dollar industry you paid to help you with your retirement planning, believed this to be true and were unknowingly ill-advising their clients.

They would look at:

- The investments you had.
- Approximate your average rate of return.
- Determine how many years you'd need your portfolio to last (basically, estimate how long you were going to live).

… and then use these figures to make your plan.

Think of it like the opposite of a mortgage. For example, you might have:

- A nest egg of $1,000,000

- Be earning an average of 6% per year
- Expect to be retired for 30 years

In this circumstance, your pre-1990's advisor would have incorrectly recommended that you could withdraw 6% of your portfolio. In fact, they might have gone so far as to recommend that you could take out as much as $72,649 per year (a withdrawal rate as high as 7.3%).

But as you'll soon find out, that would have likely been a HUGE mistake. And here's why.

The Difference Between Average Returns and Guaranteed Returns

A "guaranteed return" is exactly what it sounds like: No matter what, you'll get paid exactly the amount you were quoted for your investment.

The classic example is a bank CD (certificate of deposit). When you invest in a bank CD, the bank pays you a predetermined interest rate in exchange for you not using that money. It's as simple as that.

(Believe it or not, in the 1980's and even the 1990's, it wasn't that uncommon to find banks offering CD's with rates as high as 10%. Could you imagine locking into one of those rates today?)

An "average return", on the other hand, means that the rate reported was merely an *average* of the rates that were experienced. (To get technical, it's the geometric average.)

Stocks are a very good example where it's appropriate to report their "average return". Each day, stock prices fluctuate up and down. But at the end of the day (like you hear on the evening news), they often state something to the effect of "stocks were up by 1% today". For the common person, it's not exactly newsworthy to report each and every value that they fluctuated between.

The same is true on an annual basis. It's more useful to say that "stocks went up by an average of 10% this year" then to report which values they fluctuated between.

But therein lies the problem: **Those market fluctuations are by no means trivial!** The exact order and magnitude that your investments went up and down can have a dramatic effect on your nest egg as you withdraw money for your retirement nest egg.

This is a very real phenomenon known as "sequence of returns" risk.

Understanding Sequence of Returns Risk

To help you understand how sequence of returns risk works, allow me to illustrate the concept using the following example:

- Three people (Vince, Larry, and Mary) all retire at the same age.
- They each retire with a nest egg of $1,000,000.
- They each withdraw the same $50,000 per year for expenses.
- Their nest eggs contain the same investments: 100% stocks from the S&P 500 earning approximately 10% per year.

Therefore, after 30 years of retirement, if everything above is the same, *then they should each have the same amount of money left in their nest eggs, right?*

Wrong!

The actual values of each nest egg are as follows:

A) Vince: $529,240
B) Larry: $10,356,508
C) Mary: $5,277,407

So what gives? Why did each of them end with something different?

The one piece of information I left out was **when** each person retired ...

A) Vince: 1931
B) Larry: 1952
C) Mary: 1965

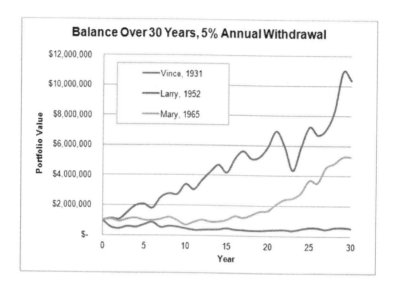

What does that have to do with it?

As you can see, quite a bit!

We'll start with poor Vince. Again, let's look at the history of stock market returns using data compiled by NYU.

Unfortunately, poor Vince retired in 1931 when stock market returns were almost -44% for the year!

How do you like that? After just one year, his entire portfolio was virtually cut in half! Because of this, any withdraws from his portfolio had effectively twice the decreasing effect as they would have had in the beginning.

As time goes on, future returns are never quite large enough to build his portfolio back up to a sustainable level. As a matter of fact, in 1937, he takes yet another devastating hit -35% which drops his balance down even further!

The end result is that his portfolio never exceeds the original balance.

Larry, by contrast, experiences a nice string of positive year over year returns during the first decade of his retirement: 53% in 1954, 44% in 1958, and so on.

As a result, his portfolio builds up strong and his withdrawals have less of an overall impact.

Mary's experience starting in 1965 is somewhere in-between Vince and Larry. She experiences both positive and negative years of returns, but the swings are much more modest. As a result, her portfolio grows slower than Larry's but better than Vince's.

Conclusion: As you can see from this example, average returns don't necessarily tell the whole story. As you're making your necessary withdraws for retirement income, **the sequence of those returns is extremely important in determining how much of your assets you'll use and how long they will last.**

Inflation Is Just As Important As the Market Returns

Market returns aren't the only thing that can negatively impact your portfolio over time.

Inflation, the tendency of everything to rise in price year over year, can also influence your portfolio in just the same way. You could almost think of it as something like a "negative" market return since the trend is for your money to be losing purchasing power as time goes on.

Similar to how we describe market returns, whenever we talk about inflation, it is often more useful to describe it as an average. For example, you've probably heard that on average inflation increases by 3% year over year.

But again: This can be a little misleading. The actual rate for each particular year may be higher or lower than this average. Just like market returns, the exact sequence and magnitude of those inflation values can impact the life of our nest egg.

How to Deal With Sequence of Returns

After reading about sequence of returns risk, you might be asking yourself: How in the world am I supposed to plan for this? How can I know ahead of time what the sequence of returns will be for the next 30 or years, and then pick a withdrawal rate that will be right for me to use?

The answer: Of course you can't know ahead of time what the markets will be. (No one can.)

But you can do this: **We can pick a withdrawal rate that is "safe".**

By "safe", I mean the following. We're going to come up with a number to use that will:

1. Give you the greatest odds of never depleting your nest egg.
2. But be high enough that it won't require you to excessively save up more than you need to.

In other words, we need to find the perfect compromise between safety and affordability.

So where do we start?

Enter a Financial Planner from California

As we said, up until the 1990's, there was a false assumption that you could simply withdraw approximately whatever average returns you were getting from your nest egg. In fact, there was one prominent figure in the media that stated if you earned 7% per year from stocks on average that you would be okay withdrawing this amount from your nest egg. (This, of course, was wrong.)

Then, out of nowhere, an unknown financial planner from California wrote an article that would change the way we thought about safe withdrawal rates forever.

Chapter 5

The 4 Percent Rule

In October of 1994, the *Journal of Financial Planning* featured an article that would come to be known as one of the most historic, often-referenced, and highly debated topics in financial planning.

At its core, the article provided us with something extremely valuable. It gave us a very simple, easy to follow guideline that virtually anyone can use when thinking about retirement.

It was the birth of what has since become "The 4 Percent Rule".

Bengen and the Origin of the 4 Percent Rule (1994)

When William P (or Bill) Bengen wrote his now famous article "Determining Withdrawal Rates Using Historical Data", he didn't set out to revolutionize the way we planned for retirement. All he wanted us to do was help us understand that sequence of returns risk was a very real problem when we're planning for retirement, and offer a better solution.

DETERMINING WITHDRAWAL RATES USING HISTORICAL DATA

by William P. Bengen

At the onset of retirement, investment advisors make crucial recommendations to clients concerning asset allocation, as well as dollar amounts they can safely withdraw annually, so clients will not outlive their money. This article utilizes historical investment data as a rational basis for these recommendations. It employs graphical interpretations of the data to determine the maximum safe withdrawal rate (as a percentage of initial portfolio value), and establishes a range of stock and bond asset allocations that is optimal for virtually all retirement portfolios. Finally, it provides guidance on "mid-retirement" changes of asset allocation and withdrawal rate.

The year is 2004. You have done a creditable job of building your financial planning practice over the last ten years. Your retirement clients are particularly well-satisfied. You have demonstrated to them the virtue of a diversified portfolio of investments to provide

WILLIAM P. BENGEN

However, you cannot help feeling a gnawing concern that you have overlooked something....

It is 2009. True to your forecast, the stock market has recovered nicely during the last three years, and most clients' portfolios have regained almost all their lost

planner into trouble was assuming that average returns and average inflation rates are a sound basis for computing how much a client can safely withdraw from a retirement portfolio over a long time.

As Larry Bierwirth pointed out in his excellent article in the January 1994 issue of the this publication ("Investing for Retirement: Using the Past to Model the Future"), it pays to look not just at averages, but at what actually has happened, year-by-year, to investment returns and inflation in the past. He demonstrated that the long-term effects of certain financial catastrophes, such as the Depression or the 1973-1974 recession, can overwhelm the averages. Such "events" cannot be ignored, and the client should be made aware of them.

In this article, I will build on Bierwirth's work, approaching it from a slightly different tack. Using the concept of "portfolio longevity," I will present simple techniques planners can use immediately in their practice in advising clients how much they can safely

After demonstrating the dangers of basing a retirement plan on average returns, Bengen presents the reader with a series of data sets designed to do one thing: *Find the greatest amount of money that you could safely withdraw from your nest egg without any fear of depleting your funds.*

48

As a former aeronautical engineer turned financial planner, he used a very data-driven and analytic approach to solving this problem. It was both brilliant and creative!

How the 4 Percent Rule Was Established

In order to find the optimal withdrawal rate, Bengen back-tested various withdrawal rates against something called "rolling periods" of market data.

To illustrate how this would work, the first simulation would start with a retiree in 1926. The calculation would find how many years it would take until the entire portfolio ran out of money. Then he'd do the same thing for 1927, 1928, ... and so on all the way up to 1976.

It's important to note that Bengen didn't just look at market returns. He also factored inflation rates for each year into the equation as well. He knew that the combination of both factors would have a profound net effect on the end result.

Bengen ran the simulation multiple times using withdrawal rates ranging from 1 to 8 percent and using different stocks and bonds ratios. As you might guess, lower rates lasted for a long time while higher rates lasted only a few years.

Any guesses which rate he decided was optimal?

Bengen's Conclusion

The take-away from Bengen's article was simple and straight-forward:

A retiree with a portfolio of 50% common stocks and 50% intermediate term treasury bonds could successfully withdraw 4.0% from the starting balance of their portfolio, and then continue to do so with inflation adjustment for a minimum of 33 years.

Hence, the "4 percent rule" was born.

So how exactly does this work? Let's say you retired with a portfolio of $1 million dollars:

- First year: You could withdraw $40,000.
- Second year: You would take out the same amount as the year before and adjust for inflation (example 3%): $41,200.
- Third year: You would again take out the same amount as the previous year and adjust for inflation (example 3%): $42,436.
- And so on.

Some rolling periods, an inflation-adjusted withdrawal rate of 4.0% worked great for over 50 years! But since we wanted a "safe" number that worked for every rolling period (no matter what the sequence of returns was), Bengen choose 4.0 percent as the optimal figure.

But That's Not All!

Although the 4 percent rule was the main conclusion from Bengen's famous article, there were plenty of other useful discoveries that his research revealed.

For example, it may interest you to know that:

- Withdrawal rates of 3.0 and 3.5% with the same inflation adjustment sequence worked for over 50 years in every data set! (Early retirement seekers, take note!)
- Asset allocation was a major influence. Increasing your portfolio to 75% stocks and 25% bonds increased most periods to last 50 years or more. But the minimum period dropped by one year to 32 years of success.
- Portfolios with stocks below 50% or above 75% were counter-productive; meaning these retirees would have ran out of money sooner than 30 years.
- If you had a secondary goal of ending your retirement with the largest portfolio possible (to perhaps leave to heirs), the higher stock allocation of 75% was the most beneficial.

At last! Someone had finally offered a way to deal with sequence of returns risk, and with tangible data to back it up.

But it wasn't until years later the 4 percent rule really gained in popularity.

The Trinity Study (1998)

In February of 1998, the AAII (American Association of Individual Investors) Journal published another important milestone for the 4 percent rule.

Three professors of finance form the Department of Business Administration, Trinity University, San Antonio, Texas, Philip L. Cooley, Carl M. Hubbard and Daniel T. Walz, had decided to conduct their own study of safe withdrawal rates.

Their approach would be almost identical to Bengen's; using the same "rolling-periods" method that he had previously used. However, rather than focus on how many years your money would last 100% of the time for a given withdrawal rate, the authors instead developed statistical probability rates for a matrix of fixed withdrawal rates (3 to 12%) and time-frame periods (15 to 30 years).

Their paper was dubbed "The Trinity Study", and you can easily Google it to find a copy. Again, the table of results they developed are well worth taking a look at.

The Trinity Study Makes Similar Conclusions to Bengen

The take-away from the Trinity Study was very similar to Bengen's:

A retiree with a portfolio of 50% stocks and 50% bonds will have a 95% chance of success of not running out of money for at least 30 years if they start making withdrawals at a rate of 4.0% and increase those withdraws with inflation every year thereafter.

More Gold Nuggets of Info

In addition to validating Bengen's earlier claim, the Trinity Study also made the following other valuable points:

- The analysis was conducted with both inflation adjusted and non-inflation adjusted returns. Even though we know that a safe withdrawal rate of 4.0% works with inflation adjustment, it was also found that a rate as high as 6.0% could be used if you DIDN'T adjust for inflation every year with a 95% chance of success for 30 years or more. (More on this point later ...)
- If you bumped up your stock allocation to 75%, your chances for 30 years of success jumped up from 95% to 98%.
- Similar to Bengen, portfolios with stock allocations below 50% or above 75% were counter-productive.
- Also similar to Bengen, the authors concluded that a portfolio of stocks closer to 75% would leave you with more money at the end of retirement.

(A quick technical note: If you're wondering why Bengen's 4% rate worked for 33 years and the Trinity Study's 4.0% rate only worked 95% of the time for 30 years, the difference was in the investments they used. Both Bengen and the Trinity Study used the Standard & Poor's 500 index for stocks. But when it came to bonds, Bengen used intermediate treasury bonds while the Trinity Study used long-term, high-grade corporate bonds.)

Again, the financial world had more validation to suggest that the 4 percent rule was the magic number to use!

Updates By Bengen and The Trinity Study

Obviously, 1994 and 1998 was some time ago. But fear not. These two articles have since been updated by their original authors.

In 2006, Bengen wrote a book called *Conserving Client Portfolios During Retirement* and revised his conclusions. Rather than generically call it "the 4 percent rule", he now refers to the minimum safe withdrawal rate as his "SAFEMAX" value. It has been raised from 4.0% to 4.5%. His revised strategy also calls for a more diverse portfolio.

In 2011, the Trinity Study authors also updated their research taking into account more recent market activity.

Here is what the revised article concluded:

- A retiree with a 75/25 stocks and bonds portfolio can now use a withdrawal rate as high as 7.0% for 30 years with a 91% success rate if they do NOT adjust annually for inflation. If you have a 50/50 stocks and bonds portfolio and use a withdrawal rate of 6.0%, your success rate increases to 98%.
- A retiree with a 75/25 stocks and bonds portfolio can use a withdrawal rate of 4.0% for 30 years with a 100% success rate if they do make annual adjustments for inflation. If you have a 50/50 stocks and bonds portfolio, that same withdrawal rate will drop to 96% success rate. Note that that's 1% more than it was in 1998!
- No surprise: Portfolios with higher stock allocations again resulted in higher values over 30 years; approximately as high as 6 times vs 3 times for the two scenarios above. If leaving money behind to heirs is a priority, then a higher allocation of stocks is in your favor.

Weigh-In's From Michael Kitces and Wade Pfau

Since its inception, many financial researchers have attempted to recreate the studies made by Bengen and the Trinity Study.

In 2010, financial researcher Dr Wade Pfau re-created the Trinity Study and found that a 4.0% withdrawal rate had increased to a 96% success rate (he did this before the revised Trinity Study was published).

Financial researcher Michael Kitces also recreated their experiment, and added some other unique perspective to the discussion. He investigated a 60/40 stocks and bonds portfolio going all the way back to 1870, and concluded that:

- Two-thirds of the time, the retiree finishes with two times their original starting balance! The median value was 2.8 times the original balance.
- Less than 10% of the time does the retiree EVER finish with less than the starting principal.

I find that second point to be especially interesting. If you are one of the lucky 90% of people who are retired for 30 years and still have more money than what they started with, then you could effectively launch into a "second phase" of retirement with confidence for an additional 30 years using a 4.0% withdrawal rate all over again!

Conduct Your Own Study for Free with FIRECalc

If you'd like to have some financial-fun on your own and see which rates do / don't work, there is an awesome free online tool called FIRECalc that will let you run your own withdrawal rate tests.

On the default screen, all you need to do is put in:

- Your desired income level,
- How much savings you have (or plan to have), and
- How many years you'd like it to last.

Then presto! You get a very noisy graph that shows you dozens of rolling periods and what sort of trend you could expect to experience.

How do you read their graph? You don't. The lines of course represent the highs and lows you would have experienced, but this is meant to illustrate the general trend of the behavior. The more interesting thing to pay attention to is the success rate that was achieved (see the text highlighted in yellow above).

I spent a little time with FIRECalc one day doing some investigation work of my own, and posted my findings in an article on MyMoneyDesign.com. Like Bengen, I found that an inflation-adjusted safe withdrawal rate of 3.5% or lower was pretty close a 100% success rate for 50 years or more!

Retirement Portfolio Success Rate							
Number of Years	Annual Percentage Withdraw Rate (Inflation Adjusted)						
	3.00%	3.25%	3.50%	3.75%	4.00%	4.25%	4.50%
30	100.0	100.0	100.0	98.3	94.8	92.2	82.6
35	100.0	100.0	99.1	96.4	92.7	81.8	74.5
40	100.0	100.0	97.1	93.3	84.4	78.2	70.5
45	100.0	99.0	96.0	93.0	81.0	73.0	70.0
50	100.0	100.0	97.9	90.5	82.1	76.8	67.4
55	100.0	100.0	98.9	91.1	82.2	77.8	66.7
60	100.0	100.0	98.8	89.4	82.4	78.8	63.4

* Success rate calculations courtesy of FIRECALC   MyMoneyDesign.com

You can go to FIRECalc and use your own numbers to see what happens. If you're feeling really adventurous, they also have an "Advanced" section where you can alter other variables such as inflation rates, stock to bond ratios, factor in Social Security, etc.

It's pretty much a financial geek's dream come true!

Conclusions - What Can We Learn From All of This?

As I've said before – the math isn't what's hard. It's knowing the "meaning" behind the numbers that will make or break your odds for a very long and successful retirement.

This is why it is very important that you understand what these values mean for you.

Let's summarize as follows:

Start with the 4 Percent Rule

Though history is no guarantee of what will come in the future, it can be argued that it can help create reasonable "corridors" for what to expect.

If you can believe this, then we find that Bengen's 4 percent rule conclusion is in fact quite safe. In fact, as we saw in the original article, there wasn't a rolling period where the retiree didn't enjoy at least 33 years of passive income; most of the time more!

Therefore, going back to our ongoing example with a $50,000 annual passive income target, if we know that a safe withdrawal rate of 4.0% will last a minimum of 30 years, then we can reasonably plan to save up a nest egg of $50,000 / 0.04 = $1,250,000.

But we don't have to stop there …

Give and Take with Inflation Adjustments

Even though the Trinity Study supports Bengen's 4 percent rule claim, it also did something Bengen didn't do: The Trinity Study provided us with both inflation adjusted and non-inflation adjusted withdrawal rates.

By considering both, we no longer get a single goal from our retirement equation. Rather, we get a range to shoot for depending on what sort of concessions we'd be prepared to make.

For example, consider the updated Trinity Study's conclusion of a safe withdrawal rate of 7.0% if you do not adjust for inflation. If you plug this value into your equation, you'll find that now you only need to save up $50,000 / 0.07 = $714,286. That's $535,714 less than what we thought we had to save before!

But aren't we going to need to increase our withdrawals for inflation every year?

The short answer: Yes. BUT, if you were struggling to save for retirement or late to get started, I'd say you could exploit this conclusion in a variety of ways.

Consider:

- At some point you will probably begin receiving Social Security payments that will help subsidize your retirement income needs. As of the publication of this book, this is currently $1,310 per month in 2016. If Social Security is only 10 or 15 years away, then could likely survive this short amount of time without making adjustments.

- You don't necessarily have to adjust every single year. Maybe you could adjust every two or three years. $50,000 will probably work just fine for you this year as it did last year.
- You also don't always have to adjust for the full inflation rate. If inflation went up by 3%, why not adjust by 2% or 1%? Remember that every percent you subtract from your inflation adjustment is like gaining another percent return on your investments.
- Your expenses will likely change as you age. A lot of research suggests that as we get over the "honeymoon" of being retired, our expenses gradually start to taper off as we adjust our lifestyles and start to develop new routines.

Increasing the Chances of Never Running Out of Money

Even if you're not struggling to save for retirement and perhaps just want the added confidence and security that your money will last you longer than what the researchers have predicted, again, you could use these findings to your advantage.

What if you plan to retire early and need your money to last a lot longer than 30 years? What if your goal is 50 years?

To start, we saw in the updated Trinity Study that keeping your portfolio closer to 75% stocks increased your success rate to 100%! But not only that, Bengen's paper showed us that it also increased the number of rolling periods that lasted 50 or more years when compared to a portfolio of only 50% stocks.

Let's say you wanted to stick to 50% stocks but still would like near 100% guarantee of success. Bengen's data also demonstrated that a withdrawal rate as high as 3.5% for a portfolio of 50/50 stocks and bonds would work for a minimum of 50 years every time!

Going back to our example, that would require a worst-case nest egg size of $50,000 / 0.035 = $1,428,571. From the Trinity Study we know that if we could find ways to make concessions on inflation adjustment, then a rate as high as 6.0% would work requiring a nest egg of only $50,000 / 0.06 = $833,333.

Again, based on what kind of adjustments we're willing to make, we now have a range of savings targets between $833,333 and $1,428,571 that would be acceptable.

In the Next Chapter

If you thought that's where the story ends when it comes to safe withdrawal rates, then please sit back down! We've got yet another interesting strategy that may cleverly allow you to need to save even less using market timing to your advantage ...

Chapter 6

Using Market Conditions for a Better Safe Withdrawal Rate

In the last chapter, we learned that the 4 percent rule was, in fact, very safe for a variety of reasons.

But if you're like me, then you were probably curious:

Why did some rolling periods work for just a little over 30 years, and others worked for 50 or more years?

Or to look at this from another perspective:

How come some periods of 30 years were able to sustain a safe withdrawal rate much higher than 4.0%? In some cases, a withdrawal rate as high as 10.0% would have worked!

While we saw that asset allocation and inflation adjustment can affect which safe withdrawal rate you ultimately choose to use, there is one more surprising and valuable piece of information that helps to answer these questions.

And just like our other tools, this information can also help us to optimize our savings goal so that we don't "over-do-it" with a too conservative plan.

How Market Conditions Can Affect Your Withdrawal Rate

In 2008, financial researcher Michael Kitces released a very popular edition of his self-published *Kitces Report* entitled "Resolving the Paradox – Is the Safe Withdrawal Rate Sometimes Too Safe?"

In this write-up, Kitces tackled the same questions we asked above: *Why do different safe withdrawal rates work some of the time?* More importantly, is there a predictable pattern?

Fortunately, the answer to that question is "yes"!

What he found was this: When you graph the safe withdrawal rates for 30 year periods against the annualized real returns for the first 15 years of retirement, the numbers aren't random. A strong correlation exists.

Remember we saw a phenomenon similar to this in our sequence of returns example with Vince, Larry, and Mary. The market returns for the first 10 years or so made quite an impact on how each of our three retirees performed.

While this is valuable information, **how can anyone predict what their first 15 years of retirement is going to look like?**

Enter Detroit, Michigan-born and Yale University professor Dr. Robert Shiller.

Dr. Shiller is credited with something called the Cyclically Adjusted PE (CAPE) ratio. Technically speaking, it's the price to earnings ratio (PE) of the US S&P 500 based on average inflation-adjusted earnings from the previous 10 years. (You will also sometimes hear this value referred to as the Shiller PE Ratio or PE10.)

How does this help us? The CAPE ratio provides us with a general indication for how the market is going to behave over the upcoming decade.

In other words:

- When the CAPE is high, it means the market is currently over-valued and likely due for a correction over the next 15 years.
- When the number is low, it means the market is currently under-valued and likely to increase over the next 15 years.

It is by no means a pin-point indicator of future events. All it does is simply provide a general sense of where the markets are more or less heading.

Now, let's apply this back to retirement planning.

Again, recalling that safe withdrawal rates can be connected to average annualized market returns, Kitces was able to show that the Shiller CAPE too had a remarkable 0.77 correlation to this data.

From there, he is able to conclude the following:

- You may use a safe withdrawal rate of 4.5% if the Shiller CAPE is greater than 20 since the market is currently over-valued and likely to have sub-par average returns over the next 15 years or so.
- You may use a safe withdrawal rate of 5.0% if the Shiller CAPE is between 12-20 since the market is currently fairly valued.
- You may use a safe withdrawal rate of 5.5% if the Shiller CAPE is less than 12 since the market is under-valued and likely to have higher than average returns over the next 15 or so years.

Brilliant! Now let's see what this does for retirement planning strategies.

Knowing the CAPE Affects Your Rate

Thanks to Kitces, we now have yet another tool at our disposal to help justify the possibility of safely using a withdrawal rate higher than 4.0% without fear that we'll run out of money. And as a result, this means we may not have to save up as much in our nest eggs or take as long to get there!

Example

Consider if you wanted to create $50,000 of inflation-adjusted passive income for 30 or more years. Using Kitces conclusions about the Shiller CAPE value being between 12 and 20, the size of our nest egg would be as follows:

- CAPE more than 20: A safe withdrawal rate of 4.5% will require a nest egg of $1,111,111.
- CAPE between 12 – 20: A safe withdrawal rate of 5.0% will require a nest egg of $1,000,000.
- CAPE less than 12: A safe withdrawal rate of 5.5% will require a nest egg of $909,091.

That's anywhere from $138,889 to $340,909 less than the original $1.25 million we first determined we'd need using Bengen's classic 4 percent rule of thumb.

Early Retirement

Another way you could apply this information is to consider what it could do to increase the longevity of your nest egg.

Let's say you wanted your portfolio to last 50 or more years. If you were going to start using the Bengen 4.0% inflation-adjusted withdrawal rate, you could seek to retire when the Shiller CAPE was on the lower end of the spectrum (below 20 or, even better, below 12). That would be an indicator that the next 15 years might go favorably for your portfolio, your sequence of returns risk would be very low, and that your nest egg would survive long after 30 years.

Combine this observation with the asset allocation and inflation-adjusting strategies we outlined in the last chapter, and now you've got several different tools you can either do more with less and really make your money last!

In the Next Chapter

While most of the information I've been sharing with you about the 4 percent rule has been reasonably positive, I must also tell you that it is not without skepticism. And for good reason ...

Chapter 7

The Safety-First School of Thought

For most people, if they were told to sit at a Black-Jack table that paid out 95% of the time, you'd have a line out the door!

But not everyone sees it from this perspective. To look at things from another way, let's pretend you had to catch a flight today. But there's a catch: 1 out of the 100 planes leaving is certain to crash.

Would you still fly?

Why Take Any Risk At All?
If during all of our talk about the 4 percent rule you've still felt uneasy about the odds, you're definitely not alone.

Everyone has a different tolerance for risk. It's a completely personal thing. For some people, a 95%

chance of success of not ever running out of money is way too high of a gamble. In some instances, even a 99% chance may still not sound good because there's still that lingering 1% opportunity for failure.

This is especially important if you have any ambitions of an early retirement. NO ONE wants to retire in their 50's, 40's, or even 30's only to prematurely run out of money and reluctantly go back to work in their 70's and 60's.

While I'm not certain that anything involving money is ever truly 100% guaranteed, there are many critics of the 4 percent rule that claim it's too unnecessarily risky, and they instead call for an alternative strategy where almost all risk is eliminated.

Safety-First vs. a Probability-Based Approach

Up until now, everything that we've been talking about with "safe" withdrawal rates comes from something called the "probability-based" school of thought for retirement income planning.

To put this in context, for every withdrawal rate we've analyzed, there is always a rate of success associated with it. There is some inherent element of a "gamble"; even if it's very small.

The safety-first school of thought takes a different approach. First and foremost, it puts the goal and certainty of retirement income before all else. Period!

A safety-first approach is not concerned with reaching retirement as quickly as possible, having the most retirement income possible, or even building the most amount of wealth. Its primary purpose is singular:

To find a way to ensure that the money you need for your basic essentials and contingencies are met under all circumstances!

Secondary priorities such as leaving money behind to heirs or wealth growth are held to a much lower priority; or in some cases dismissed altogether. These would be considered discretionary or legacy priorities, and are far behind the first two.

Because there can be no risk, it is not acceptable to use a variable asset source to generate income. Translation: A retirement nest egg based on market returns is far too risky! In the safety-first approach, there is *no such thing as a safe withdrawal rate*. To truly have 100% certainty, the income source must be guaranteed.

The safety-first school of thought is not something new. It has been around since the 1920's with the research of people like Frank Ramsey and Irving Fisher. In recent years, one of the bigger advocates for the safety-first approach is financial researcher Dr. Wade Pfau. You can learn more about a safety first approach by going to RetirementResearcher.com and reading these two posts:

1. What is a Safety First Retirement Plan?
2. Two Philosophies of Retirement Income Planning

Could the 4 Percent Rule Be Unsafe?

Is there any truth to the 4 percent rule or a probability-based approach being flawed?

Unfortunately, going forward, there may be some chance for uncertainty.

As Dr. Wade Pfau put it in the NY Times:

Because interest rates are so low now, *while stock markets are also very highly valued, we are in uncharted waters in terms of the conditions at the start of retirement and knowing whether the 4 percent rule can work in those cases.*

It's true. Google "Federal Interest rates over time" and you can see for yourself that they've been at a historic low for quite some time.

Dr Pfau was also part of a paper from 2013 in the Journal of Financial Planning with co-authors Michael Finke and David M. Blanchett called "The 4 Percent Rule Is Not Safe in a Low-Yield World." In it, they warn that if current bond returns don't spring back to their historical average until ten years from now, up to 32% of nest eggs would evaporate early.

Of course, these points are only a matter of opinion since the future always remains uncertain.

In support of a traditional probability based method, Michael Kitces argues that:

The 4 percent rule was built around some rather horrific bear markets of the past already. Do we necessarily know or expect that the next one will be so much worse than any of the other terrible historical bear markets we've seen?

How Do You Use the Safety First Approach?

Because the primary objective for retirement is to build a safe and secure income floor for the entire retirement planning horizon, safety-first advocates recommend you consider pensions, bond ladders, and income annuities when meeting these requirements.

Once the foundation is laid for your basic income needs, you can then invest the rest of your money in more volatile assets (like stocks) that will fund your discretionary purchases.

Example

For the sake of argument, let's consider what would happen if you took your entire nest egg balance and purchased an annuity.

Using a simple generic online quote provider, at the time of this publication, we find that a 45 year old couple could purchase a $1 million dollar immediate annuity from an A++ rated insurance company that would pay just over $40,000 per year.

That's not too bad! Notice that we're getting basically about the same 4% return on investment that we would have received with the 4 percent rule. Of course, the exception is that here the money is guaranteed for life. You will never stop receiving payments for as long as you're alive (and the insurance company remains in business).

The bad news is that if you and your spouse get hit by a bus tomorrow, then the money is all gone. The annuity payments stop, the money stays with the insurance company, and that leaves you with nothing to leave behind to your heirs.

(Note: You can buy annuities that leave behind some or all of your initial investment to heirs. However, the payout is considerably less.)

Recall that in the safety-first philosophy, legacy endowments like this are a secondary consideration. In this example, the primary goal of secure, guaranteed payments for life has been achieved.

How Does This Change Our Target Nest Egg Goal?

The reason I have included this chapter in our discussion is because, again, I think that it is absolutely vital to understand the meaning behind the numbers you plan to use for determining your nest egg goal. Whether those meanings have positive or negative connotations, it would be irresponsible not to consider the topic from all perspectives.

While I tend to lean more towards the probability-based school of thought, I don't think you can (or should) dismiss what the safety-first approach is trying to accomplish: Confidence. Therefore, there is no reason you can't combine elements of both strategies to come up with a winning, power-house combination!

Example

Let's say that you plan to retire by age 50 and would (again) like to shoot for a passive income goal of $50,000 per year. But this time you'd like at least half of our income ($25,000) to come from a guaranteed source. This way, applying an element of safety-first logic, you'd always know that your basic needs will be met.

Using the same online, generic quote tool as above, we find that we'll need at least $550,000 to purchase an immediate annuity from a reputable source that will bring in this level of income.

To fund the remaining $25,000 of our desired income, we could then switch to a more probability-based approach. Using Kitces withdrawal rates as an example, we'd also need an additional:

a) $555,556 assuming a safe withdrawal rate of 4.5%, or
b) $454,545 assuming a safe withdrawal rate of 5.5%

This means that our total nest egg goal should be anywhere between $1,004,545 and $1,105,556 in order to execute this strategy.

(Note that these figures are not that far off from the goals we concluded we could use in the previous chapter.)

Conclusions

As I said, I included this chapter to give you broader perspective on retirement planning security in general.

Ultimately, the decision on how you'd like proceed is yours. Only you can define what "safe" really means to you.

If you are more comfortable with risk, then probability based methods may be more suited for you. But if having an absolute guarantee that you will always receive money every month no matter how the markets behave, then perhaps considering some or all parts of a safety-first philosophy may not be out of the question.

A Word on Annuities

When it comes to annuities, **please proceed with caution**!

Annuities are known for having excessive:

1. Up-front fees
2. Hidden fees
3. Fees that no one ever tells you about

(I think you get the idea ...)

Though annuities are some of the oldest retirement planning products out there (dating all the way back to the time of the Romans), the modern versions have a notorious reputation. In addition to the issue with fees, they can also be laced with complicated rules that make it difficult for the average investor to understand. When it comes to investing, **understanding what you're getting yourself into is always the first step!**

While I used the link above to get a simple estimation for what an annuity pays out, please keep in mind that it is really not that simple. Before an annuity provider will give you a concrete offer, you have to apply for one and provide them with a lot of personal information. Just like life insurance, a variety of factors such as your age, spouse, lifestyle habits, and the terms of the contract itself will determine what kind of an offer you will receive.

No matter how smart you think you are with money, when it comes to annuity, I'd advise seeking the guidance of a **trusted** financial professional before you ever sign the dotted line.

In the Next Chapter

Now that you've learned probably everything you could ever want to know about safe withdrawal rates, it's time we turn our attention back to the first variable we considered in this whole retirement equation: Defining how much income you really think you will need.

As you'll soon see, optimizing this figure can lead to knocking hundreds of thousands of dollars off your end goal.

Chapter 8

Optimizing Your Retirement Income Needs

Remember in Chapter 2 when we came up with a "number"? This number was meant to be some guess at how much you'd need each year to cover your expenses.

We're going to revisit that topic. And as you can probably guess, there's definitely a good reason to do so. After an exhausting discussion of safe withdrawal rates, one thing should be clear to you:

No matter which one you choose for your plan, every dollar you think you will need for retirement will be an amplification of what you will need to plan to save in your nest egg.

Think back to our simple retirement equation. The math is easy to see! Take the 4 percent rule for example:

Every $10,000 extra of retirement income that you think you will need will cost you the time and energy to save up an extra $10,000 / 0.04 = $250,000 in your nest egg.

So why not be strategic? Let's turn this concept around and use it **our** advantage!

For every $10,000 of retirement income that you can afford to do without, that's $250,000 less that you need to save in your nest egg.

It's true! We've been generically using $50,000 in every example so far as our target retirement income. But could you be just as happy with $45,000 or $40,000? What about even less?

Crunch the numbers. A retirement income target of $40,000 using the 4 percent rule drops our nest egg savings target down from $1,250,000 to $1,000,000. Considering how many years of saving that could knock off of your plan, I'd say it's worth looking into.

In this chapter, we're going to address a pivotal decision that lies before you: **How much money do you *really* think you will need for retirement?**

Though initially you might have your doubts about being able to live on less, it might be beneficial to know that this concept of reducing your expenses is the cornerstone to many successful early retirement strategies. Have a look for yourself!

How Early Retirement Bloggers Live On Less

Many of the top early retirement bloggers were successful not because they acquired millions of dollars in some extraordinary or unique way. They were able to do it because they simply found a way to not "need" as much money as the typical person.

One very extreme example of this is Jacob Lund Fisker from the website and best-selling book *Early Retirement Extreme*. Jacob was able to retire before the age of 30 after only 5 years of working by getting his annual spending down to below $10,000 per year. Knowing what we know about the 4 percent rule, a retirement income like this would only require a mere nest egg savings of $250,000! Though his approach is certainly not for everyone, it illustrates the extent to which a lower income need can affect your overall plan.

Another good example is the blogger Mr. Money Mustache (real name Peter Adeney). MMM (as he's called) is another popular retired-by-age 30 character that publicly boasts about enjoying an annual budget of just

$24,000. His retirement only required a savings of $600,000 to pull off.

Along the same lines are Jeremy and Winnie from the website with the unusual name Go Curry Cracker. They too utilized the 4 percent rule to retire in their 30's with $40,000 per year in anticipated expenses. However, they make their dollars stretch farther by living for extended periods of time in places with lower cost of living than the U.S.

One of my favorite examples of a successful early retirement is that of Robert and Robin Charlton from the book "How to Retire Early". They were able to save almost $1,000,000 from scratch in just 15 years and retire before age 45 with a projected retirement income of $40,000.

There are many, many other examples of other bloggers who have used similar strategies. The forum Early Retirement.org also has thousands of stories from people who have either achieved financial freedom or are on their way there.

Redefining the Word "Fun"

A lot can be done with less than you think. This is especially true when you read through many of the articles from the early retirement blogging community.

As you really analyze their stories and listen to their philosophies, you come to understand that part of what helps make each of their plans a success is all in how you define the word "fun".

Often you'll hear them redefine fun as:

- Traveling to exotic, lower cost of living locations
- Spending time with family or friends
- Taking their time to accomplish projects around the house
- Being active outdoors
- Volunteering
- Playing a sport they like
- Learning a new hobby
- Tons more!

If your definition of fun is spending is buying the latest gadget, dining out to an expensive meal every night, and traveling to exotic resorts, then that's fine. Again, your retirement should be designed for you and no one else.

But understand as a result you'll be faced with a much steeper challenge. The math simply doesn't change. If we generalize that you think you'll need a generous $200,000 of retirement income per year, then the 4 percent rule quickly shows us that you'll need a whooping $5 million for your nest egg. Are you prepared to make that happen?

Spending Changes As You Age

Even though we've been using a "fixed" figure for our retirement income in nearly every example, it may be useful to know that this may not be the case. According to David Blanchett from Morningstar, **inflation-adjusted spending in retirement gradually decreases over time** (unless health-care costs cause it to rise again in life's final years).

He quantifies this as follows:

Households spending $50,000 at age 65 decrease their real spending by about 15% by age 80; the drop hits 20% by age 85. For those spending $100,000, it's 20% by 80 and nearly 30% by 85.

Lowering Your Expenses

Being more frugal does not necessarily mean cutting back or denying yourself certain luxuries. Most of the time it simply involves the act of tightening up your finances and working down your expenses.

For example:

- Could you have your house paid off before you decide to retire? If you've got a $1,000 mortgage payment every month, eliminating it would slash $12,000 from your annual needs. That's **$300,000 less to save up in your nest egg**!

- Could you drive your car for an extra year or longer? Or buy a used car with cash? If you can afford to avoid a $500 car payment, that will save you an extra $6,000 per year. Again, **that's another $150,000 less you need to save!**
- Can you cut down on your household energy costs?
- Get a cheaper cell phone plan?
- Get a better price for your insurance coverage?
- Find a cheaper health care provider?
- Eat for less?
- Drive for less?
- Buy fewer clothes?
- Hold out a little longer to get the latest gadget?
- Scale back your discretionary purchases?
- Negotiate lower rates for you bills?

And many others! Finding creative ways to save money is something that I feel so strongly about, I used it as the central theme for one of my ebooks "Save MORE, Earn MORE".

What You Should Do

Go back to the retirement plan that we wrote out earlier in Chapter 2 and think about how you could have some more fun for less.

- *What would be some of the activities that you get involved in?*
- *What sorts of things would you find value and enjoy learning?*
- *What could you be doing to improve your health and psyche?*
- *How can you give back to yourself, your family, and your community?*

Think also about some of the ways that you could strategically cut back on your regular, everyday expenses to try to squeeze more out of your bills.

Put this all together and come up with a new retirement income goal.

Is this a number that you could truly live with?

Finally, talk openly about your plan and everything it entails with your spouse. In order for it to work, the two of you both need to be on board and work together as a team. Be honest with each other and discuss what each person's vision of the future may look like.

Remember: Similar to Chapter 2, the goal is not to slash your needs and drive this number down as low as it can possibly go.   It's simply to consider if there is any opportunity for optimization that you may not have previously considered.

In the Next Chapter

Now that we have a more refined idea of what our retirement goal looks like and what our nest egg goal will be, it's time to get down and dirty with saving!

Here's how we're going to do just that.

Chapter 9

Reach Your Goal More Quickly By Saving BETTER!

Now that we've came up with reasonable and sensible numbers that we can use for your personal retirement plan, there's only one thing left to do ...

... Get there!

Yes, it's time to put "the pedal to the metal" and do everything in our power to achieve financial freedom as efficiently as possible. Fortunately for you, this happens to be the topic of at least two of my other ebooks as well just about every blog post I publish on MyMoneyDesign.com.

Though the following is not a complete list of money saving strategies by any means, I do consider them to be some of the more useful methods you can use.

Enjoy!

How to Save Your Money Better!

Follow these tips and I guarantee you'll knock years off of your retirement saving plan!

1-Always Save Your Money Tax-Deferred

Tax-deferred saving (i.e. savings where you get to avoid paying taxes until a later date) is BY FAR your best choice to really turbo-charge your savings.

How so? Because of the simple fact that you're putting more money in your pocket instead of giving it all to Uncle Sam (i.e. the government).

Say, for example, that you're in the 25% tax bracket. For every dollar you save, you really only keep $0.75 because you give $0.25 away to the tax-man. But with tax-deferred savings, you get to keep the whole $1. That's the equivalent of 33% more savings than you would ordinarily get to keep in a regular, taxable savings or investment account.

Though that may not sound like a lot at first, over time this can really add up to hundreds of thousands of dollars in extra money for you! (More on that below.)

You can start taking advantage of tax-deferred savings by either signing up for your company's 401(k) program and/or starting an IRA with an investment broker (like Vanguard).

Don't worry about the rule where you can't withdraw your money before age 59-1/2. We've got lots of tips and tricks to get around that in my other ebook "Early Retirement Solutions: How to Unlock Your Savings Before Age 59 ½ Without Penalty".

2-Get FREE Money with Employer Matching
If your employer offers any sort of matching program for your 401(k) or other retirement fund, do everything in your power to take full advantage of it!

To not do so is to simply give up an opportunity to cash in on free money – perhaps thousands of dollars each year!

Though the majority of employers will offer 50 cents to the dollar as a matching incentive, some employers are especially generous and will do a 1:1 match against your contributions. That's literally a 100% return on your investment, all for simply doing nothing more than saving like you should be doing!

Talk with your HR representative to find out the full details of what your employer offers.

3-Start as Early as Possible!

Compounding returns can cause your money to grow exponentially over time. But to really put them to work and get the most out of them, you need to start investing your savings as early possible. By doing so, you'll give them the most amount of time they need to save the greatest chance for a successful outcome.

4- Save MORE!

The ultimate factor in savings is quite simply how much YOU decide to save.

My advice to everyone is always strive to save as much as you can. The more you do, the more you take advantage of each of the factors above.

For example, if you were to save all the way up to the current maximum IRS 401(k) contribution limit of $18,000 this year, that would mean you would have avoided paying almost $4,500 in taxes! That's a lot of extra money going right back into your pocket.

5-Invest in Stock-Based Assets

When you do invest, make sure a large portion of it is in stocks or funds that have stocks (such as mutual funds or ETF's).

As we learned above from Bengen and the Trinity Study, portfolios that are heavily weighted in stocks (near 75%)

tend to have better chances for sustainability and produce larger yields over time. This is especially important during your accumulation phase of life because our goal is to maximize the size of your nest egg before you are ready to retire.

You really don't need to look any further than a passive index fund that follows the S&P 500 to suit your needs. Dozens of financial greats from John Bogle to Warren Buffet have supported that these simple, low-cost funds are a great way for the average investor to outperform the vast majority of activity managed funds out there.

6-Lower Taxes with Capital Gains & Dividends
If you do have to save your money in a taxable savings or investment account, do it the smart way and go for assets that will yield capital gains and/or dividends (such as common stocks).

These types of assets are taxed at a much lower rate than ordinary income (such as employment wages or interest).

7-Tax-Deferred College Savings
As a parent, it can sometimes be difficult to balance saving priorities for both retirement and your children's college. This is where a 529 plan can be useful.

A 529 plan is another tax deferred plan (similar to how an IRA or 401(k) works) but with the intention of funding your child's college expenses rather than your retirement. You can generally find these available through your local state website.

8-Tax-Deferred Health and Child Care
If your employer offers them, make sure you're using FSA's (flexible spending accounts) or HSA's (health savings accounts). These plans will give you the opportunity to use tax-free money to cover your health and daycare expenses.

9-And Many More!
By no means does the list stop there.

Every time I go on the Internet and browse through a dozen blog posts or so, I'm always astonished by the amount of creativity and ingenuity people have when it comes to finding new ways to save more money.

I invite you to go online and see for yourself. There's always something new to learn.

What You Can Do
Ask yourself: *Am I doing everything on this list and really taking advantage of every opportunity that's available to me?*

Let's start with your 401(k) or IRA:

- Do you even have one or both of these?
- Are you saving enough to get the full employer match?
- Are you saving as much as you possibly can to max out your tax-deferred savings?

Speaking of your employer:

- Are you taking full advantage of that FSA or HSA?

If you're saving your money in regular savings account:

- Why aren't you maxing out your tax-deferred savings first?
- Are you investing in assets that have lower tax-rate capital gains or dividend opportunities?

What about your spending?

- Just like in the last chapter, are there things you could be doing to work down your debts more quickly?
- Do you have a family budget?
- Are you paying for things or services you don't really need?
- Are you checking Amazon or the Internet to make sure you're always getting the best price?
- Are you continually auditing your bills to make sure you're getting the best rates possible?
- Are you questioning every expense?

Please don't feel overwhelmed. Rome wasn't built in a day. You can work on as many or few of these actions as your efforts permit.

The race for the finish line is always the same. Ultimately, you determine how fast you'd like to get there.

Chapter 10

Summary

So there you have it!

Your path to financial freedom, the lifestyle you'd like to live, and the size of the nest egg you'll need to make it all happen is really just based on two very important things:

1. How much money you think you'll need each year.
2. How to go about withdrawing that money from your nest egg with the confidence that it will likely never run out!

As you've seen, there are many different opinions and philosophies on what "good numbers" are for each of these variables. Ultimately, like many things in life, a lot of how you will approach this topic will depend on your specific needs and what you feel comfortable with.

Fortunately, we've learned a lot of useful information that we can put to good use along the way! Let's review.

So … How Much Do We Really Need to Save?

Let's do a quick recap using our ongoing $50,000 retirement income target example.

Going back to Chapters 3 and 4, we started off showing you how a savings account earning 2% would require a very large nest egg of $2,500,000. A portfolio of all dividend stocks earning 3% would require $1,666,667, but would not give you much diversification against market risk.

In Chapter 5, things got a little bit better. We learned from Bill Bengen and the Trinity Study about the meaning behind the 4 percent rule. This knocked our goal down to $1,250,000 with inflation-adjusted withdrawals.

In addition, we also learned a very important lesson about inflation. If we are able to make some concessions about the way we adjust for inflation, then our target may be even less. Taking this to the extreme, if you could live without inflation adjustments (say until Social Security kicks in), then you could use a withdrawal rate as high as 7 percent and save as little $714,286.

In Chapter 6, Michael Kitces taught us that we can improve upon the 4 percent rule and make inflation-adjusted withdraws as high as 5.5% when the market is under-valued using the Shiller CAPE as a barometer. This would reduce our nest egg savings target down to $909,091.

In Chapter 7, we learned about the safety-first approach to retirement planning and some of the certainties it can guarantee. Though it does generally require a larger nest egg and could potentially mean giving up some of your financial legacy, it would satisfy that fundamental need to know that you will never run out of money, no matter what the market conditions are.

In Chapter 8, we were again reminded that retirement planning starts with YOU. Every dollar you think you will need in retirement is practically 25 times what you need to save. Therefore, you should be very conscious of your needs and really try to consider how you might be able to do more with less.

If you could reduce your retirement income target by 20% from $50,000 down to $40,000, then your nest egg savings target would drop from $1,250,000 to $1,000,000.

What If You Want to Retire Early?

If you're planning to retire early and need your money to last you for more than 30 years, then many of the tricks we've learned along the way could be useful.

For example:

1. We know that for many rolling periods, the 4 percent rule worked for 50 or more years. Therefore, if we're willing to accept a little more risk, then we could simply start there and create a passive income of $50,000 with annual inflation adjustment using a nest egg savings goal of $1,250,000.

2. If we wanted to boost our certainty from 30 years to 50 years, then we could look back at Bengen's 1994 article and reduce our withdrawal rate down to 3.5%. That would also create an income of $50,000 per year with inflation adjustment requiring only a nest egg of $1,428,571.

3. Why not have your cake and eat it too! Since the Trinity Study showed us that "non" or "partial" inflation adjusted withdrawals increased your odds of success, you could use a higher withdrawal rate if you're willing to cut back on your inflation adjustments. I back-tested some data and found that an early retiree could effectively re-create the safety of a 3.5% safe withdrawal rate while taking out as much as 4 percent per year and decreasing their annual inflation adjustment by 1.5%. That's a decrease in nest egg savings of $178,571!

The Power Combo!

If you'd really like to show your retirement savings whose boss, why not combine ALL of the strategies we've covered thus far?

Imagine the strength of your plan if you were:

- Holding more of your portfolio in stocks.
- Minimizing how often you adjust your withdrawals for inflation.
- Minimizing the rate by which you adjust your withdrawals for inflation.
- Retiring when the Shiller CAPE is 12 or less.
- Reducing your anticipated expenses at retirement.
- Considering other ways you may be able to reduce your retirement income needs.

The possibilities for optimization are endless!

Emphasis on the Word "Planning"

One of the last thoughts I'd like to leave you with is something that was stated by the Trinity Study authors:

*The word **planning** is emphasized because of the great uncertainties in the stock and bond markets. Mid-course corrections likely will be required, with the actual dollar amounts withdrawn adjusted downward or upward relative to the plan. The investor needs to keep in mind* *that selection of a withdrawal rate is not a matter of contract but rather a matter of planning.*

(Bengen echoed a similar cautionary in his article as well...)

I think it's important to recognize that "planning" is nothing more than a tool. You can have the absolute best-laid plan, and it might have a 99% chance of certainty. But no matter what, there will always be that 1% chance that something will change. Something might go wrong. There might be something unknown.

Don't let this stop you!

There are no shortage of naysayers who will be very quick to try to discourage you and point out the flaws in your plan. As a blogger, I get this all the time with many of the ideas I write about.

My advice to you is: Don't listen. Seek out the facts, make your plan, and adjust it as you see fit. Even if you never exactly hit all the numbers you forecasted, I still STRONGLY believe that you're going to be FAR better off than if you had had no plan at all.

There's an old saying that goes "Failing to plan is planning to fail". As I've mentioned before, retirement planning shouldn't be something that happens by circumstance. Good fortune and wealth don't happen by accident. They are often the product of very simple actions such as saving, investing, and thinking ahead. The magnitude of the those outcomes will be directly related to the quality of your plan.

But as humans with evolved brains, we can do something that goes beyond simply putting numbers into a spreadsheet. Like the Trinity Study authors and Bengen suggest, one of your weapons when it comes to planning is to be ready and willing to make changes as needed. Human beings are hard-wired with the instinct to survive. And when it comes to your finances, your recourse should be no different.

Bengen never once intended for anyone to continue making 4 percent annual withdraws if the market took an extended nose-dive and running out of money was eminent. The 4 percent rule was only ever meant to assist you in constructing a well-intended plan for the future. Once you're actually there, you don't necessarily need to follow it to absolution. You can adjust and play defense as you deem appropriate.

After all, it's your money.

So for now, while there is plenty of good information to work with, I again encourage you: Create your plan. Talk about it with your spouse. Optimize it and make a good one! But don't too hung up on any one detail. As long as you're willing to change and adapt, you're going to be just fine.

Until then, keep on saving!

Thank You!

Thanks again for reading this book! I sincerely hope this advice helps to greatly improve both your financial situation and your quality of life.

Those two reasons were exactly the reason why I created my blog **My Money Design**. I take the tagline "designing financial freedom" to heart!

With every new post on My Money Design, I promise to share with you every new trick that I learn, whether it's a new idea for generating wealth, avoiding taxes, or simply getting one step closer to financial freedom. Please sign-up for free updates, and as a special thank you **we'll send you a complimentary copy of our eBook "How to Plan Your Financial Freedom"**. We'd love to have you be a part of our community!

Also, before you go I'd like to encourage you to **please take a moment and please leave a review for this book on Amazon**. Doing so will not only help me but it will also help other people just like yourself know which ebooks are the best ones to read. Thank you in advance!

Sincerely,

DJ Whiteside (aka MMD)

http://www.mymoneydesign.com

More Great eBooks from DJ!

Early Retirement Solutions: How to Unlock Your Savings Before Age 59 ½ Without Penalty

Retire Sooner! How to Optimize Your Plan to Achieve Financial Freedom

Save BETTER! Use the Secrets of the Wealthy to Retire Early, Create Passive Income for Life and Achieve Financial Freedom

Save MORE, Earn MORE! 21 Easy and Practical Ways to Save More Money for Your Retirement and Other Financial Goals

64247229R00069

Made in the USA
Lexington, KY
02 June 2017